KARL, CHESTER,
and a sheep named
SHARON

**Bedtime Stories for a
Lifetime of Leadership - Volume 1**

SCOTT MCGIHON

© Scott McGihon 2020

ISBN: 978-1-54399-877-1

eBook ISBN: 978-1-54399-878-8

WHAT'S INSIDE

AUTHORS NOTE

Have you ever wanted to lie in bed, and not get up? When it seems like the weight of the day is telling you it would be better to pull the covers back over your head and not get out of bed?

Each day, people around the world wake-up, and — depending on if they are "morning" people or not — attack the day with varying degrees. Except all too often, the "attack" feels like it has been reversed, and it's the day, or sometimes even the world, that is the one doing the "attacking".

While we may feel alone in those times life seems to be throwing everything it has at us, the truth is we are not. These challenges are faced around the planet daily, as Karl, Chester and Sharon, along with a surprise visit from Jack, soon remind us.

In all the parts I have played in my life — husband, parent, coach, entrepreneur, student and employee —, it's become very clear to me that we all face challenges each and every day. And I choose the word "challenges" carefully, instead of "problems/troubles/obstacles/etc", because I know the power words have not only when they are spoken or read, but even more so when they are thought. These challenges can oftentimes seem overwhelming and daunting, and when left unattended or unaddressed, can grow to become barriers that keep us from experiencing and enjoying all we have right in front of us.

Depending upon the season of life you are in, Karl, Chester, Sharon and Jack's encounters may or may not seem directly applicable to you, but if you open your eyes to those around you, you will find many going through what each character is going to experience.

As you enjoy the following stories, open up your mind and heart to what is being said and felt; you may find answers for you, or for someone else, that you did not even know you were looking for!

THE LONELY
SHOPPING CART

This story was born out of a conversation I had in a men's group I started a few years ago. We were talking about those funny little quirks that maybe only a few people notice but spark immense curiosity. My friend Joe mentioned shopping carts in parking lots and the decisions some people make when they are done with their carts. While we had a hilarious time talking about it, and then sharing photos later, it planted a seed inside me. Here is a story from a point of view not often heard: the shopping cart's!! Enjoy!

Karl the shopping cart was excited.

Today was the day!

Recently, he had not only been painted a sleek black color, but he had also been outfitted with a red plastic hand bar (for pushing).

And to complete things, he had been blessed with a shiny red seat with hinges, so little kids could sit on him; and when they weren't in the seat, it could be flipped up to make sure things did not roll out and onto the ground.

But the best of all—what made him really proud—were his wheels. Dark, glossy black, they ran smooth and silent and spun all the way around, so people could push him easily in any direction.

But with all of that, what made today so special and exciting?

Last night, he had been delivered to the grocery store, where he knew his job was to help people with their shopping by being big, quiet, and easy to push.

He was so excited to help people and do his part to feed their families, that he almost could not stand it.

From the stories he had heard told by the people who put him together, it was just like Christmas morning, when every little boy and girl wakes up and runs downstairs to see what Santa brought during the night.

Yes, today was the day that he would finally become and fulfill all he was designed to be. And the day turned out to be just as amazing and wonderful as he expected.

Except...except...except he noticed that sometimes he was left by himself.

He knew that the only time this happened was when he had been able to do exactly what he was built for.

But it also seemed as though sometimes people didn't care and would just leave him.

But he also knew that every time that happened, eventually someone came along and rounded him up with all his brothers and sisters, and brought them back to the front of the store, where they would eagerly wait for their next turn.

It was a little bit of a shadow on an otherwise amazing day. The laughter and joy he heard from kids as they pushed him, walked beside him, or even sat on his special shiny red seat—oh, how great and joyful that was!!

And so, every day, Karl would "wake up" in the morning, all tucked in nice neat rows and columns with his brothers and sisters, ready and excited to start the day, help so many, and fulfill his destiny.

But as time went on, Karl started to notice that the time it took to be collected grew longer and longer and, more and more, he was left in all sorts of odd places.

Sometimes he was left in the middle of a parking space, which made no sense, as that was where cars were supposed to go. If a car could not park, then people could not get out and use Karl.

Sometimes he would be left, with his front wheels kind of dangling over a curb, between the front ends of two parked cars. This also made no sense, as then no one could get him out without bumping into one or even both of the cars.

Sometimes he would get a push from the person that had just used Karl to shop for food for their family. This push would often leave him close, but not quite in, the cart corral, where all shopping carts were supposed to be collected.

And then there were the times Karl did not like at all.

These were the times when he would be left in the far reaches of the parking lot, sitting by himself.

Which is where Karl found himself today.

The day had started with the usual excitement.

He was overjoyed when a family came in and grabbed him, and spent a long time in the store filling him up.

And, like everyone else, once they paid for their groceries, they loaded the bags back into Karl, and wheeled them all out to their car.

But once they got to their car and unloaded all the bags from Karl, placing them inside their car, they did what Karl liked least of all.

They gave him a slight push, and then drove away.

And there Karl sat and waited, ready and eager to be used again.

And he sat.

And he waited.

And he watched the shadows on the ground move, as the day went on and the sun moved through the sky.

As the day continued with no one coming to get him, Karl got a feeling he had never experienced before.

He became lonely.

As the shadows got longer and the night approached, the parking lot became emptier and emptier.

Then, almost in an instant, it was completely empty.

Empty, except for Karl, who was left in a distant corner, all by himself.

And after what seemed like a very long time, the night passed and gave way to a new morning.

Karl was still lonely, not to mention slightly damp from the morning dew, but he was also hopeful.

Because although you could not see it from the way he now looked—kind of dirty, paint faded a little bit, chips in his red handle— he still wanted to be what he was designed to be.

But sitting by himself during the night, he started to think about all the not nice things he had heard people say, and he started to believe them.

Even worse, he had begun to imagine bad things people would say when they saw him!

And so Karl had spent the night alone with his thoughts. Which is never a good place to be when you are feeling sad and lonely.

So he waited as the morning grew brighter, still alone with his thoughts.

Eventually, the people who worked in the store arrived, and a little later one of them came out and walked through the parking lot, collecting all the carts that had been left out overnight.

But even as he was collected, and brought to the front of the store, this didn't make Karl feel better.

He was thinking only of all the bad things people had said and the things he imagined they would say.

So, Karl was not the happy, joyful cart he wanted to be.

And he sat there, lined up with all the other carts, waiting for the store to open, but not really caring.

Now, by divine intervention, next to Karl, with all of the other carts, was an older cart named Jake.

Jake had been at the store a looong time. So long, in fact, that he was the oldest cart there, and no one knew exactly when he was first brought to the store.

Jake could tell Karl didn't feel so good about himself.

He knew Karl had spent the night in the parking lot by himself, and, having spent many a night out there alone, he knew what Karl was thinking.

He also knew this was an important time for Karl, and that if something or someone didn't take the time to help him, Karl would have a very rough time and an uncertain future.

So, while all the other carts were just sitting there waiting for the customers to arrive, Jake began talking to Karl.

He wasn't talking with Karl, because Karl was doing his best to ignore him, almost as though he wanted to sulk by himself, lost and alone in his negative thoughts.

But Jake kept talking. And the reason why was very simple.

Years before, he had been in the same position as Karl, and another cart had taken the time to talk to him.

And as Jake kept talking, Karl finally began to listen.

What he heard was not in the slightest bit what he expected.

Jake told Karl that he had a decision to make.

Karl could sit around feeling sorry for himself and get older and crustier, believing all the bad things people said or he imagined they would say.

Or, he could choose to do something else and continue to grow to all he had been designed to be.

Jake helped Karl see that if Karl always relied on what other people said, and what other carts may say, if that was what drove him every day, then his journey would be a long one, and he might never feel truly happy or joyful again.

But if Karl held fast to what he had first thought when he arrived at the grocery store (and what he felt deep down inside of him), then the limits put on him by others would not keep him down.

Jake said that many people try to make you feel bad about yourself, because they feel bad about themselves, and the only way they think they can feel better is to make someone else feel worse.

Jake also said that far too many people believe only the negative things, because they are so easy to believe.

This is especially sad because it keeps them from becoming what they were designed to be and become.

Karl, wanting to believe, but still being held back by those earlier bad thoughts, asked Jake how he knew this.

Jake replied, "Because another cart a long time ago said the same to me and challenged me to keep my head up and move forward, never listening to the things that would keep me from being who I am designed to be."

And as Jake continued, he said, "And you know what? That cart was right. Too many times I started to listen to what other people said about me, and it made me feel bad. And when I started to feel bad, that's when I started to doubt ever becoming what I am supposed to become."

Karl asked Jake what he did then, because he knew Jake had been around a long time, longer than all of the other carts, and that kids loved Jake.

Jake replied, "I realized I can't fix people, even if they say they want to be fixed. I can only do my best to bring joy to them. And to bring joy to them, well..."

Karl couldn't stand it!

Just when he thought Jake was going to solve all of his problems, he stopped talking!

Karl pleaded with Jake. "Please, please, please tell me. Tell me how you bring joy to people every day. That's all I want to do, and I know that is my calling."

Jake looked at him, almost as though he was trying to make up his mind.

Finally, after what seemed like forever but was really only a few moments, Jake spoke, and this is what he said.

"To bring joy to people, I know I have to continue to become what I am designed to be. And I am designed to be a cart, but not just any old, run-of-the-mill cart."

"I am uniquely created."

"But just because I am uniquely created, that does not mean things will come easy for me."

"Bad things will happen. Bad things will be said to and about me. And bad thoughts will creep inside my head."

"But I can fight all of that bad stuff, and move forward to where I am called to be."

"And the way I do that? It's two pieces, really."

"I believe, and mean truly believe, that I am destined for some-thing."

"And this may be hard to believe, but that's the easier of the two parts."

At that, Jake paused, knowing what was coming next, but also knowing it was the thing most people say they want to do, but are reluctant to put into action.

Karl, kind of jumping up and down, but never leaving the ground (picture a shopping cart trying to jump, and you will get the idea), begged Jake to continue.

"You want to know the second part? You really, really want to know?"

"The second, and equally important part? I work on myself every day."

"I don't wait on and rely on others to fix my wheels. If they start to squeak, I take that squeak and make it fun."

"Who cares if my wheels don't run straight? They may take me someplace new, or in a direction I never thought of, and when they do, guess what? I bring others with me, to a place they have never been to, and a place they never thought of going to."

"This may seem weird. Why would anyone want to go a different direction than they planned? It doesn't seem to make sense, and seems so impractical."

(If Karl had a head, he would have been nodding it, because that's exactly what he was thinking).

Jake stopped suddenly, looked at Karl, and asked him, "Why were you created?"

Karl was a little shocked that Jake asked him a question, and because he was shocked, he blurted out "To help people!"

And Jake replied, "Exactly. If that is what you truly believe, you are exactly right."

"But Karl, how can you help people when you are feeling so sad?" Jake continued.

"How can you make their day any better when right now all you want to do is be mopey?"

As Karl began to say, "But it's not my fault!" he realized the truth and wisdom of what Jake had said.

And in that moment, there was silence.

Finally, Karl said, "I get it, Jake. If I always wait for others to do things for me, to make me feel better, then nothing will get done."

"I need to make a choice every day."

"I need to choose and decide who and what I will be every day."

"When I do that, I will be on my way to becoming what I am designed to be."

"I will be the one people look to constantly, and I will be able to bring joy to everyone around me."

"And that is who I am and how I was designed!"

As Karl finished, Jake grinned a silent grin. He knew Karl was going to be okay. Actually, Karl was going to be better than okay: he was going to flourish and thrive.

He knew that every day would bring new challenges, and some days would be better than others, but Karl had inside of him all he needed to continue growing and becoming.

And Jake also knew that while there would be more nights and days when Karl was left in some random spot in the parking lot, and that Karl's wheels would squeak and go in different directions, he knew the greater truth.

As long as Karl held onto making a choice every morning, he would be the joyful, amazing cart he was designed to be.

So the next time you are the grocery store, take a look around the parking lot. You may just see Karl and Jake, sitting out by themselves. Or maybe you will see another cart that is just waiting for a kind word of support, maybe a push in the right direction, just like Jake gave to Karl. And you can be that difference maker, helping another cart become all it is designed to become. It all starts with deciding to be who and what you are designed to be and knowing you have in you the power of choice.

Choice not only for you, but for all of those around you.

CHARGED WITH PRIDE

Z ap!

Crackle!!

Zzzzzzzzzzzzzzzzzzzzttt!

Chester the charge felt amazing. He was humming and thrumming and moving faster than the eye could see.

All around him, the air was electric.

He moved from place to place, from line to line, from walls to wherever, and he felt so free!

Everything and everywhere he touched came "alive" and started humming and thrumming in its own way.

The only shadow on an otherwise amazing day and life was that each "touch" left him feeling a little drained.

But that feeling of being a little drained always left him soon, and without fail he always felt recharged.

He was so used to being filled back up almost immediately that he did not really think about it, and he assumed this would always be the case.

And as he went through each day, filling others with his touch, he became more and more confident and secure.

As his confidence grew, and he continued to share the energy and power he carried with others, his thoughts soon became boastful and filled with pride.

Chester soon started to think and believe no one else could do what he did!

And so, over time, Chester began to think only of himself, and how he looked, and what he did.

These pride-filled thoughts soon turned into selfish thoughts, and once he started down this path, it was not long before he became convinced that he was the best thing ever, and that everyone else needed him, and only him, and what he could do.

But that was not the only thing Chester thought.

No, as his mind became more and more occupied with pride, it was not long before an even more corrupt notion joined his pride.

What was it, you may wonder?

What was it that took its place in Chester's head?

Chester thought, and came to believe, "If everyone needs me, and I already have me, then clearly I have all the answers, and I don't need any one."

And this dangerous, sinister thought soon became how he looked at each day, and at each touch in the day.

Until, one day, Chester felt different.

He experienced something he had never experienced before.

He no longer was humming and thrumming, and he certainly was not moving faster than the eye could see.

He didn't feel like lightning, and he absolutely did not feel super-charged.

But even worse than that, and far scarier than anything he could have imagined, he had a feeling he had never known and did not know he could feel.

Chester felt drained!

Drained in a way he had never felt. Drained in a way that felt so wrong, so awfully different, that it took him a while to realize what it was.

And while he was trying to figure it out, he knew one thing for certain.

He not only wanted to get rid of the feeling as soon as possible and in whatever way possible, he absolutely never wanted to feel it again.

What was this feeling that left Chester at a loss?

That made him feel alone and—even though he did not want to admit it—helpless?

Chester believed he had forgotten how to charge up.

With that thought, Chester began to feel sorry for himself.

And as he sank further and further into what was becoming desperation, he became more and more scared.

Finally, when the feeling was almost overwhelming, he cried out, "What is going on? Why is this happening to me?!!"

To which there was no reply.

And, for a long time after, still no answer.

Which left Chester feeling mostly alone, with his only companion his increasing desperation, until finally, after what seemed to Chester to be forever, but was really only an hour (when you move like lightning, time seems really slow), he heard a voice.

And that voice?? He knew that voice!

But he could not remember who the voice belonged to.

So Chester cried out frantically, "Hello? Who's there?"

"Do... do I know you?"

Chester waited for a reply for what seemed like a really long time.

Finally, he heard the voice start speaking again.

The voice, the voice that he knew he should know but could not remember, said, "Chester, I can tell you don't remember me, but you should."

"Just as you touch and contact so many every day, you and I meet daily as well."

At that, Chester became very confused, a little more frustrated, and also more than a little upset.

In a loud voice, that was almost but not quite a shout, he said, "What do you mean?"

"We meet each other every day?!"

"I don't know what you are talking about!"

"I don't know who you are!"

"I spend every day doing good things, helping others, and now I feel tired and drained, and you tell me we know each other?!"

"Who ARE you?!!"

The voice, again after what seemed like a very long time, answered.

Oh, all the things it said. The light it shed on Chester. The passion it had in its voice.

But most of all, the sound of truth in all the things it said.

The voice said, "My name is Barry. Barry the battery. And I have to tell you some things, Chester, so that you can make a choice."

Then the voice (which Chester now knew was called Barry the battery, or just Barry) fell silent, waiting for Chester to make a choice.

After a brief moment, Chester said impatiently, "Alright, yes, whatever."

"Yes, tell me what YOU think I need to know."

At which point, Barry began to talk. And the first thing he said? It was not what Chester ever expected—not in a million years would he have expected it.

"Chester, I forgive you. I forgive you, and it hurts me to see you feeling this way."

Now, this confused Chester even more.

Forgive him?! What had he done wrong??

But before Chester could speak (which was a small miracle—remember lightning speed?), Barry continued.

Barry told Chester that all the things Chester did every day were amazing and so needed.

And he should be proud of how he helped to make others feel. (Chester thought, "Helped? I did all of that. That was all me." But he kept quiet.)

Barry spoke on. And what he said caused time to stand still for Chester.

He told Chester that while he did great and noble things every day, and that his impact on the world could not be denied, that he had forgotten that he was part of a larger team.

A team that really never got attention in the way Chester did.

And you know what?

The team was fine with that. After all, being part of a team means you do things to help the team succeed, not bring attention to yourself.

And the team that Chester was part of was amazing.

There was Barry the battery, of course. But also on the team was Charlie the charger, Eddie the electrical cord, Oscar the outlet, Lucy the power line, and Petey the power plant.

Each of them was super important and critical to the success of the team.

Petey worked night and day to produce electricity, which he then handed off to Lucy.

Lucy carried the electricity produced by Petey all the way to Oscar, who waited patiently for Lucy's constant deliveries.

Oscar in turn gave the electricity to Eddie, who was plugged in and connected to Oscar.

Eddie then carried that precious cargo of electricity to a variety of places, but for this team, he carried it to Charlie.

Charlie then transferred the power to Barry.

And Barry?

Barry stored this power until he was reunited with Chester, and was able to give it to him, thus recharging Chester for his daily missions.

When the work of the team powered up Chester, he was then able to transfer it to so many others.

And, Barry continued, this happens all over the world, with so many other members of the Electric company, everyone working together to chase the shadows away and make the world a bright place.

But, recently, all members of their team had begun to feel as though Chester didn't care about the team.

That it was all about Chester, and no one else.

And while they did not need to get applause or claps on the back, they did want to feel they were all valued.

All they wanted was every now and then to have Chester say "thanks," especially since they knew he received so much recognition every day.

A simple thanks for the team doing its part.

Then, Barry finished talking with this final thought.

"You have a choice to make Chester."

"The choice is very simple."

"You can continue to sit feeling mopey, all alone with your pride. You can even choose to wallow in self-pity and never feel the way you love to feel again, gradually draining out until there is barely any charge or any of Chester left."

"Or you can take a moment and do something that should be so simple, and so easy, yet may feel like a tremendous challenge."

"And that is to thank those every day that help you just as you help others, and be filled with gratitude, and the power of your team."

With that, Barry fell silent.

And Chester did something he had never done before.

He sat still.

He thought of all the lives he had touched.

All the joy, electricity, and power he had brought to others.

The feeling of excitement and energy he delivered everywhere.

But most of all, he thought about what Barry had said.

ALL of what Barry had said.

And he knew why Barry had forgiven him.

But mostly, he thought of the two choices Barry said he could make.

And, while it seemed obvious which choice he should make, he still struggled to make it.

To admit he needed help from others, that was such a strange and foreign thought to him. Why, when others looked at him, all they saw was a clean and finished product, humming with pure energy.

But, deep down, way deep down inside him, he knew Barry had spoken the truth.

And he knew that saying thanks was such a little thing to do, but such a big thing to receive.

It was kind of the opposite of forgiveness, which is sometimes so hard to give, but so easy to receive.

Not coincidentally, they were both things he wrestled with.

Because, while saying it should seem like a little thing, a little thing that he knew would bring great joy and rewards, it was also admitting that he was not in charge.

No, not **IN** charge, but **A** charge.

With that thought, Chester felt something loosen inside of him.

Almost like a crust breaking off him, he felt more free and electric than ever before.

And, much like scales falling off of his eyes, he could see things he had never seen before.

He couldn't wait to tell others of what he had discovered, as he brought energy throughout the world to them.

He knew he had found a truer, much better source of energy!

An energy that would power up not only him, not only the ones he met, but an energy that would electrify the entire planet.

But before he could do all of that, before he could go out and change the world, there was one thing he needed to do first, one "world" he needed to energize before all others.

And so he thanked all the members of the team one by one.

Barry

Charlie

Eddie

Oscar

Lucy

Petey

He not only thanked them, he asked them to forgive him, which they each gladly did.

Further, he asked them to each hold him accountable in the future, as he knew that just like making and carrying electricity, he could not do it on his own.

And so the entire team was able to come together, and bring both energy and a powerful message to the world.

A message of teamwork, forgiveness and gratitude.

And a message that you now have and can bring to all of those in your world.

As you reach the end of the story of Chester and the energy team he is part of, take a moment to think about what team(s) you are part of.

Are you a parent?

Are you a son or daughter?

Are you a coach?

Are you on a sports team?

Do you work with others?

Are you in a classroom?

There are so many places, and so many people that silently cry out for recognition.

There are so many teams we are all **A part of,** that we sometimes forget it and become **apart from** our teams.

But what if we each took a moment every day to find someone who is part of our team and offered a simple "thanks" for what they do, and how they help us to be successful?

Maybe it's the teachers and staff at school.

Maybe it's your classmates.

Maybe it's a co-worker.

Maybe it's your coaches and teammates in sports.

Maybe it's your child's coaches and their teammates in sports.

Maybe it's the checkers, baggers, etc. at the grocery store.

Maybe it's the mailman, or a delivery driver.

Once you stop, think and reflect for just a brief moment, and you may be overwhelmed with how much we all have to be thankful for, and how many we have to thank.

Start with one, and energize your "world" to energize all of ours.

PURPOSE UNRAVELED

It was the end of another day, and Sharon let out a long and somewhat loud sigh.

She had spent the day with the rest of her flock, moving through the pasture where they stayed, slowly going from one end to another, just as they had the day before, and the day before that, and the day before that, and—well, you get the idea.

And Sharon had sighed, because she was tired.

No, not tired as kids get after playing with friends and toys all day long, nor as grown-ups experience after exercising.

Those are good ways to be tired!

No, she was tired because she felt as though she had nothing to do.

But it was more than that.

As Sharon thought, she realized why she felt the way she felt and why she had sighed the way she had sighed.

It was not so much the previous few days of doing the same thing.

It was not even the fact that she had been doing the same thing all her life, since she had grown from a lamb.

And it wasn't that she didn't like her friends or the pasture where they roamed and grazed.

No, the more Sharon thought about it, the more she became convinced that the reason she felt the way she did, and had sighed the way she sighed, was simple, but it was also a little scary.

She knew—she was not sure how, she just did—that tomorrow, the day after that, and the day after that, and so on, would be exactly the same as today.

Sure, it might get hot; it might rain; it might snow in the winter; new lambs would be born and become sheep—but, really, everything would be the same.

And by being the same, there would be no change, which sounded absolutely dreadful.

So Sharon let out another sigh as she began to think through why this bothered her.

And as she did so, she came to a startling conclusion.

The reason she felt this way? It all seemed so pointless.

That what she did every day, it really didn't matter.

That she was just another sheep on the planet, among millions of sheep on the planet.

The word that popped into her head at that moment was one she had never thought of before, but it instantly seemed to be the right one.

Insignificant.

Sharon's heart sank when she thought of this word.

If who she was did not matter, then tomorrow looked pretty boring and monotonous, not to mention the days and weeks that would follow.

And so Sharon meandered aimlessly, lost in what she thought was a trap of dullness and routine.

Now, as Sharon had been lost in her thoughts and sighing, feeling somewhat sorry for herself, she had not noticed that, in her meandering, she had fallen behind the rest of the flock and was lagging behind even the oldest and slowest of the sheep.

But Buck had.

And who was Buck, you might ask?

Buck was a sheepdog.

But not just any sheepdog.

Buck came from a long line of sheepdogs. In fact, his family had been at the same farm and all of its pastures for many generations.

They were all proud of what they did, but they were especially proud of the things that went unnoticed.

Sure, they kept the sheep together, and moved them around from place to place in the pasture.

And they definitely protected the flock from any other animals that would try and do them harm.

In fact, Buck's family was so well-known in the area around the farm, that most animals that might want to eat sheep knew to stay away or things would not go well for them.

And while all of that was good, it was what Buck and his family did inside the flock that they were so proud of.

Buck as usual had been watching all of the sheep, but lately he had been keeping an extra eye out on Sharon.

He had seen the signs of her not being happy and content, long before Sharon even knew they were there.

Buck knew that what Sharon was going through was something that a few sheep a year experienced.

He knew that Sharon had to get to the point where she wanted to make a decision before he could really help.

And with Sharon now lagging behind all the other sheep, Buck knew it was time.

Buck knew the danger of feeling insignificant, as though what you did and who you were did not matter.

33

But he also knew something powerful and simple, and he was eager to share that with Sharon; at the same time, he moved with the wisdom and timing that had been passed down to him by his parents, and their parents—you get the picture.

So Buck made his way down to the flock, and as he came up to Sharon he said, "Hi," and slowly drew her into conversation.

A conversation Sharon did not want to have—it's easier to feel mopey and sad for yourself—but one that Buck knew she needed.

And the longer Buck talked, the better Sharon listened, and the more she talked too.

Buck said he knew Sharon was feeling sad and tired, and that she had started to think everything was kind of pointless.

He told her he knew that she felt as though she didn't matter, and that each day in the pasture felt like she was in a cage and would never get out.

And, most importantly, Buck told Sharon that while her feelings weren't special, SHE was!

When Buck told her that, Sharon was confused, and got a little upset, but Buck kept on speaking, and what he said helped calm Sharon down very quickly.

Her feeling of being insignificant was important — like who she was and what she did, like all of that was pointless — but that was not what made her special.

No, said Buck, what made Sharon special was something she could not see.

He told her that she had made, and would continue to make, a huge impact on the world outside the pasture.

Which completely confused Sharon, almost completely replacing her feeling of being upset.

He asked Sharon whether she remembered every spring, usually about a month or so after it stopped snowing, when she and all of the other sheep got their yearly haircuts.

She said yes, and she did not think about it much, because it felt a little weird to get all of her thick, fleecy coat taken off, but that it also felt good not to carry around so much extra weight and insulation as it started to get warm.

Buck explained that people called that "shearing" and that all of Sharon's fleece was collected.

But it was what Buck said next that stopped Sharon in her tracks.

Buck explained that her fleece, after it had been sheared, was used to make clothing for people, and that Sharon's fleece each year was enough to make five sweaters for people!

Five sweaters a year!!

And it was these sweaters, Buck said, that kept people warm when it was cold, kept little kids healthy, and also made people feel better each day, because the sweaters made from Sharon's fleece, and all the other fleece in her flock, made especially beautiful sweaters.

These sweaters, Buck said, were not only extremely popular, but were so important in keeping so many people alive and healthy.

At that, Buck fell silent.

He knew that the next few moments were important.

It was important that Sharon make her decision.

She could keep feeling mopey.

She could continue believing that she was insignificant, that any and everything she did amounted to nothing.

Or she could realize she made a huge difference in the world, a difference she had never thought of, in a world she did not really even know existed.

And in that world, people she did not even know depended upon her, and trusted she would continue to bring them comfort and joy.

And so Buck sat, watching and waiting.

He was concerned, because Sharon's response would not only impact her, not only impact those people that came to depend on her even though they did not know her, but it would have a "ripple" effect throughout the entire flock.

And that ripple effect could be something amazing, or it could be draining.

Whatever her decision, Buck knew, things would not be the same in the flock.

And as Buck watched, he saw Sharon's answer before she even spoke.

It started with a little smile; not the kind of smile you have when you eat something really good, but the smile that comes from discovering something that brings you joy in a way you did not expect.

She stood a little taller, with a posture of pride.

She lifted her head, and she waggled her fleecy little behind.

And then she spoke, looking directly at Buck.

"Thank you, Buck."

"Thank you first for taking the time to talk with me."

"Thank you for your kindness and wisdom."

"Thank you for always watching out for me and my family, and all the members of our pasture flock."

"But, most importantly, thank you for thinking of me."

"Thank you for helping me to see that I do make a difference in a way that I never knew existed."

"Thank you for letting me see I am special, and that I have always been special, even though I did not know it."

"Thank you for revealing to me that I am not insignificant, and my life does have great purpose—that each day I have is important, even if it does not seem like it in the moment."

"That there are so many that I do not even know, and that don't know me, that are counting on me and who I am created and designed to be."

Finishing up, Sharon said, "I will always be grateful for this day, Buck, and each and every day that follows."

"Some days may be brighter and sunnier than others, and some days may be especially rainy, but I promise I will make each day count, being grateful for the day, instead of trying to find a reason to not be happy."

"And I will be forever joyful, knowing who I am and continuing to grow and become all I am designed and intended to be."

With that, Sharon turned around, and bounded gleefully back into the middle of her flock, eager to make the most of the day that was left.

Buck watched the flock file into the barn where they slept, and he smiled again, knowing Sharon was going to be better than okay.

Sharon was going to be amazing, and so would everyone in her flock.

As you come to the end of this brief moment in time with Sharon and Buck, take time to think.

Know that, like Sharon, you are uniquely designed and that you have a great purpose inside of you.

Know that your purpose has already begun to come out, and it wants to keep growing and flourishing.

You have the power of choice to let it continue emerging or to bury it.

This is a choice that will determine your joy and fulfillment in life.

And a choice that will continue to impact so many people both in your flock and in the world outside your flock.

Take the time to think about being Sharon.

And take the time to look around you, and see if you can be someone else's Buck. Together, we will all change our flocks, and change our worlds.

JACK, AND THE ART
OF WINNING

J ack was fast.

He knew it.

His parents knew it.

His friends knew it.

Everybody at school knew it...you could safely say *everyone* knew Jack was fast.

And because Jack was fast, you know what he did a lot of?

Besides getting from one place to the next very quickly, finishing his homework, and inhaling his food like he was part vacuum — which are all sometimes useful — Jack did something most wish they could do, but rarely experience.

And that one thing, among so many others, that set Jack apart?

Jack won.

Jack won a lot.

In fact, Jack won so much it seemed like he never lost. And it seemed that way because he never did!

It was so widely known how fast Jack was, that when he was entered into anything, the expectation quickly became the real race/contest/meal, whatever it was, would be for second place.

And it had been this way for a very long time.

It had been this way for such a long time it seemed like it had always been this way.

Sure, there was a time when Jack was very, very young, and just learning how to get about that he was not the fastest around, but that time was so long ago that the idea of Jack always being the fastest and being the only winner was not really wrong.

This feeling of being the fastest one around? Jack loved it!

And winning? Who doesn't like to win?! Everyone loves a winner!

The attention winners receive, and all the prizes, trophies, and ribbons, those are all very cool.

In fact, Jack had been winning for so long, and had so many of those prizes and memntos, that most were simply stored away.

All of his speed, all of his victories, all of the accolades and attention, all of that was so much fun, and it seemed like a dream come true.

Except...except...except recently.

Recently it seemed like every race, every victory, every bit of attention and everything that went along with it, all had started to become a little different.

What was that difference? It was hard to put a finger/paw/foot on it.

Jack still went fast.

He still beat everybody and won.

Still, something seemed to be missing.

And that is where we pick up the story of Jack, and the art of winning.

Another race, another win. Just like yesterday, and the day before that, and pretty much every day before that.

Jack had finished with not only the win, but had again finished far ahead of everyone else in the race.

As usual, Jack had celebrated. He could not help but be excited when he won (who can?), and since he won every time he was excited a lot!

So, he had done his standard jumping up and down, moon walking in circles, and pointing to himself repeatedly, even as the others were still finishing.

But as Jack ended his celebration, he saw that for the first time ever, no one was around him to join in.

This was strange, because there was always someone, usually a lot of someones, ready to congratulate him and help him celebrate.

Although, as he thought about it, there had been fewer and fewer recently.

"Oh, well" he thought, "I guess everyone has something else going on, maybe they are sick or something." And so Jack grabbed his trophy, and headed home.

But even as he left, holding his trophy, thinking they should probably just go ahead and start engraving his name on all the trophies in advance, Jack still felt something was not quite right.

It was kind of like a feeling of being just a little off, like when you put your shirt on backwards, but that was not quite it either.

So, Jack just shrugged his shoulders, and continued home, wanting to get some rest before his next race in a few days.

The next race day came, and Jack eagerly headed to the course.

Even though he knew he was going to win, he still got excited about going to the races...the thrill of being fast, of being first, of being around all his friends, he loved all of that!

And as he began to warm-up for his race, he started talking with his friends and fellow racers.

Or rather he started talking at them, because he was so excited.

But again, he noticed something a little strange. Everyone politely listened for a little bit, but then quickly turned to someone else to talk with them.

Pretty soon, Jack found he was left talking with himself. Which was weird, and a little unsettling.

But it was race time, which meant it was winning time!

Which is exactly what Jack did.

And as he started his traditional celebration, he saw that there was no one around him again; in fact, everyone was on the other side of the race area, all talking with each other, leaving Jack by himself!

When Jack saw this, he got mad.

He thought "I cannot believe them! ALL of them!"

"I thought they were my friends."

"I thought they liked me."

"Now they won't talk with me, or spend time with me, just because I won?!??!"

And so he grabbed his trophy, and left everyone, stomping his feet in frustration and anger.

On the way home, he said to himself "If that's how they want to behave, then I will show them!"

"I am going to not only win the race tomorrow, but I am going to win by so much they have to pay attention to me!!"

"Yes, that's it, that's how I am going to show them, and make them like me and want to be around me again!"

And all through the night, as he tried to sleep, one thought ran through Jack's head.

He was going to be better and faster and win by more than ever, and give everyone no other option except to like him and want to be around him.

Morning came, and Jack jumped out of bed, eager to get to the race and starting line, but even more eager to put his plan into action.

Can you guess what happened next at the race?

Jack won! And he won by so much it was truly amazing.

And Jack was extra-excited, because everything was going according to his plan.

Except, after the race, it seemed like his sure-fire plan fell apart.

He was all alone again in his celebration.

No one even said congratulations; it was almost as if Jack was not even there!

And this made Jack even madder, to the point he could almost feel his heart hardening against everyone else.

Then he had a thought, a thought which he grabbed hold of immediately.

What was that thought? Why, it was a simple thought.

A simple, mean-spirited thought.

"I'll make them pay," thought Jack.

"I'll make them pay for the way they are making me feel."

"If they think I have been winning by a lot before, just wait!"

And so, as I am sure you can guess, Jack went out in the next few races, and took his winning and domination to a new level.

Yet, after every race, despite how much he won by, and how much attention he tried to get through some very creative celebrations — you try moon walking on your hands —, no one so much as even looked at him.

Which made him madder and madder, and continued to harden his heart, until it felt like he had a stone in his chest.

Until finally, the day came that Jack never thought would come.

No, he did not lose. In fact, he won by so much it was almost as if everyone did not even start the race.

But after the race, when it was time to celebrate, that was when things changed.

Jack started off, jumping up and down, doing cartwheels in circles, pointing to himself, but guess what?

His heart wasn't in it!

Now, you could say his heart wasn't in it because it had turned to stone, and you would not be completely wrong.

But the real, and larger reason? Jack was lonely.

He had finally gotten to the point where he realized celebrating by himself all of the time was no fun.

And because celebrating by himself was no fun, winning had also become no fun.

In fact, it seemed as if it had become like a weight, a real heavy weight, hung around his neck.

So what did Jack do?

He sat down and cried.

Sure, he tried to hide the fact he was crying; he did not want to look like he wasn't brave, or strong, or heroic, but he still cried.

And sure enough, soon the others at the race noticed.

And it would be great to tell you that they all came over and comforted Jack, but unfortunately that did not happen.

Some of them, so bitter and upset at the way they felt Jack had treated them race after race, actually started laughing and pointing at Jack.

Which did not help anyone, and made Jack feel both sadder and madder at the same time.

Jack wanted more than anything to get up and leave...no, he wanted to get up and run away as fast as he could, but it seemed like he was so tired and had no strength, so he just stayed there, and tried to not listen to what everyone was saying and doing.

Eventually, the moment came when everyone left.

And Jack was finally alone, as the shadows grew longer and longer, and the light grew fainter and fainter.

All alone, so no one could see how he felt, and see him looking so sad and dejected.

Or so he thought.

But in the stillness of the late afternoon, Jack was startled to hear someone call his name.

Not only was he startled because he had thought everyone was gone, but he was also startled because it had been a very long time since anyone had called his name, or even spoken to him.

Thinking about this made him even sadder; so much sadder, in fact, that for a moment he forgot someone had actually called his name.

But that moment quickly passed when he heard his name called again.

And as he slowly lifted his head, looking in the direction of where his name was coming from, in the dusky light he saw the outline of someone.

He thought he recognized the shape, but he still could not quite make out who was there.

And since Jack really did not feel like talking with anyone, he lowered his head again, hoping whoever it was would take the hint and go away.

A hope that quickly went away when he heard his name called again.

"Jack'", called the outline or silhouette, "Jack, what seems to be the problem?"

"Why are you crying?"

And in that moment, something seemed to snap inside Jack.

Maybe it was his tears.

Maybe it was his anger.

Maybe it was a combination of everything he was feeling, leading to confusion and frustration.

Or maybe it was simply that no one had talked with him in such a long time.

But whatever it was, it seemed like all of his frustration, sadness and anger kind of bubbled up, and erupted out of him like a volcano.

"Why am I crying?!!??", cried Jack, not even bothering to deny he was actually crying.

"Why am I crying?", he repeated.

"Maybe it's because everyone has been so mean to me."

"Maybe it's because it seems like no one likes me."

"Maybe it's because it feels like everyone is jealous of me."

"Or maybe it's because everyone that I thought were my friends have abandoned me!"

And after Jack was done with his outburst, he felt tired.

No, more than tired, he was exhausted.

And as Jack sat there, collapsed on the ground like a puddle, he waited for an answer.

He waited for what seemed like a very long time.

He waited in the quietness and silence for what seemed like an eternity.

And just when he thought that maybe he had imagined everything, and that no one was really there, he heard the voice start to speak again.

What it said was completely unexpected.

"Jack," said the voice, "Jack, do you really think everyone has been trying to make you feel bad?"

"Do you think that everyone is out to get you?"

"Do you think that no one cares about you?"

"Or," continued the voice, "Do you think any of this is because of the way you have been treating everyone else?".

When Jack heard the last question, he could not believe it.

Any other thoughts that may have been building inside him disappeared instantly.

And he went from mostly sad to mostly mad in a heartbeat.

"Who are you?!" Jack demanded.

"Who are you?!!!" Jack repeated, this time very angrily.

"I can't believe that in this moment, you are trying to make me feel even worse, trying to make me believe all of this is because of something I've done!"

"I can't even see you, and I don't know who you are."

"But I know you are wrong, and that you don't know what you are talking about!"

And again, as Jack finished, he felt completely drained and exhausted.

And again, there was nothing but silence.

Silence that seemed so big that it covered everything, and made time stop.

A silence that hung heavily, like a blanket, until finally Jack heard a rustling sound.

And as Jack picked up his head, which he had dropped in tiredness, he once again saw a silhouette. A silhouette that started moving towards him in the last bit of sunlight.

A silhouette that he thought he knew, no, that he knew he knew, but he could not put a name to.

Finally, as the outline and shape grew closer to Jack, he realized who it was.

And it was someone that was probably the last person Jack ever expected to see, especially at this time.

And the shape started nodding its head, because it could tell Jack finally recognized who he was.

Jack tried to start talking, but could not really make any sounds except those of surprise...you know, "uh", and "err", and "uhmm".

But after a few moments, Jack settled down a bit, and was able to talk.

"You're Harry," said Jack. "Harry the hedgehog".

""I used to watch you all the time when I was younger. You were the best at everything! And every race I saw, you always won!"

"You were my hero, and I wanted to be you more than anything!!"

And Harry, who had been nodding his head at all Jack said, looked straight at Jack as Jack finished talking, and said.

"That's right Jack. I am Harry the hedgehog. And you know what, if you keep up what you are doing, you will be me!"

"And that is something I would not wish upon anyone."

Now this was extremely confusing to Jack.

And since he was so surprised and exhausted, he just blurted out what he was thinking.

"What do you mean, Harry? And is it okay if I call you Harry?"

And at this Harry kind of chuckled, and nodded his head that yes, Jack could call him Harry.

"I wanted to be like you more than anything Harry. You were my idol."

"You were fast, faster than not only every other hedgehog, but faster than any other animal!"

"You always took home the best trophies, you had a dream life, you had commercials, you hung out with all the famous people, everyone looked up to you."

"As a matter of fact," Jack went on, "As a matter of fact I had your poster in my room when I was younger. I would go to all of your races that I could, and the ones I could not get to I read about the very next day!"

"Who wouldn't want to be you?!! That seems like a dream come true!"

All at once, Jack stopped, aware that he had been talking so fast that Harry could not answer.

As he sat there, looking up at Harry who was still standing, the afternoon shadows gave way to the night, and the ground was lit up with the light of the very full moon.

Harry slowly lowered himself to the ground, to sit across from Jack, still not saying anything.

Until finally, Harry began to speak.

And what he said astonished Jack.

"Jack," said Harry, "I'm sorry."

WHHHAAATTT?!?!?! thought Jack.

He's sorry? For what??!!!!

But before Jack could say anything, before he could really get the thoughts that were swirling around inside his head out, Harry continued.

"Jack, I am so sorry for what I did, for you looking up to me, and wanting to be me."

"I am sorry this is the path you started on."

"But Jack," Harry continued, " I am so grateful I am here now, and am so happy for you that there is still time for you."

Okay, wait a minute, thought Jack.

He is sorry and grateful for me wanting to be him? Weird.

But even stranger is the whole "still time for you" thing. What does that even mean??

As Jack ran these thoughts through his head, he became aware Harry was just sitting there; he had stopped talking and was looking at Jack.

Almost like he knew what Jack was thinking.

And Jack, never comfortable with that awkward silence that can happen sometimes when people are talking, decided to start talking himself.

"What do you mean?," he asked.

"Why are you sorry for what you did?"

"And what does still time for you even mean?"

Again, there was silence.

Silence that continued until Harry spoke.

"Jack," said Harry, "Jack, I have been watching you for a long time."

"For a very long, long time."

(Jack thought this sounded a little strange, but did not say anything).

"And Jack, at first I liked what I saw."

"And then I loved what I saw."

"You're a winner, Jack."

"And you should be very proud of all that you have done, all you have accomplished, all the races you have won, your amazing gift of speed and competitiveness, you should feel real good about all of that."

"But," Harry continued, "But you don't."

"Here you have been absolutely crushing everyone in every race, and instead of celebrating with others, you are sitting here crying in the dark, all alone except for me, a washed up former racer that almost no one remembers."

WHOA! thought Jack. That's a bit much, even coming from someone who had been his idol.

"Jack, before you say anything, let me speak."

As Jack nodded his head, Harry kept going.

"I was a lot like you. Except as a rabbit you already are gifted with amazing abilities, to which has been added even more speed."

"All of this has made you into the racer, no, the winner that you are."

"But it's not enough just to win anymore, is it?"

(JUST to win anymore? That's a strange thing to say, thought Jack).

"When there is no one to celebrate with, no one to high-five, it all seems kind of lonely and empty, doesn't it?," Harry continued.

"At the end of the day, all you are left with is a bunch of trophies and ribbons, news clippings and results, which really don't mean all that much in the end."

And as Harry kept talking, Jack found himself nodding his head in agreement.

"Jack," Harry went on, "You are at that point, and you don't even know how or why you got here."

"It seems like it happened almost overnight, like you woke up one day to a bad dream that has only continued to get worse."

"And I know that feeling all too well, because I lived it, ignored it, and am still paying for it."

Now that's an unsettling thing to hear, thought Jack, and one that although in one way it made sense, in another it really didn't.

What does all of this mean, Jack ran through his head, *why is Harry telling me all of this and what does he mean he is still paying for it?*

And as Jack sat there thinking, Harry waited.

He waited because he could tell Jack was running a multitude of thoughts through his brain, which he knew was a good thing. And that when Jack was ready to talk, IF he was ready to talk, he would.

And so they sat, as the moon got brighter, so bright that it started making shadows of its own.

Until Jack, kind of shaking his head as if to clear his thoughts, realized that Harry had not spoken for a while.

So Jack, full of so many questions, but also still full of awe for his hero that sat on the ground before him, stammered a bit before blurting out the questions he had.

"What do you mean?"

"Why do trophies and all of that stuff not mean anything?"

"What do you mean you are still paying for it?"

"And why are you telling me all of this?"

And as Jack finished, silence once again seemed to surround them, making it feel like they were the only animals alive in the world.

After what seemed like a long time, but was really only a few moments, Harry spoke.

"Jack, let me answer your questions in a way that will make sense."

"But to do so, I am going to have to ask you some questions along the way."

"And these questions may be easy to hear but hard to answer; still, they are the only way we can get to the end."

"Is that okay?"

And Jack, now both anxious and curious, nodded his head yes.

"Okay, good" said Harry, "That's real good, but I want you to remember that this is something you have asked for."

"Because you may hear some things that you don't want to hear, and you may find out some things that you thought you never wanted to find out; it may get hard at some points, but if you will stick with me and trust in me to the very end, perhaps you will find a way to change things, hopefully for the better."

(*Uhhh*, thought Jack, *this seems a bit scary. And "perhaps find a way to change" and "hopefully"? What ever happened to "we will" and "absolutely"?*)

Harry went on.

"Jack, like I said earlier, I know how you are feeling, I know what you are thinking, because I also went through it."

"I was the fastest ever, at least until you, and no one ever beat me."

"I collected so many trophies and ribbons that I started just leaving them wherever, even using some of the trophies as trash cans."

"And along the way, I got real popular. So popular that everyone knew my name, and wanted to be around me."

"And pretty soon, all the people around me told me how great I was, how I was the best, how everyone else did not even belong in the same race as me, that they were just wasting my time."

"And soon I found myself surrounded by people I didn't really know, but who told me how great I was."

"Which was awesome, or so I thought, because who doesn't love to be told they are great?"

"But all those strangers, who only seemed to appear when I was winning, they helped to push out my friends, people I had grown up with, and people I had raced with for so many years before I started to become famous."

"But notice I said helped push out, because they only continued what I had unknowingly started."

"Jack, have you ever heard the phrase 'winning isn't everything, it's the only thing'?"

And Jack nodded his head, yes, he had heard of it, in fact it was a phrase that made total sense.

"I thought so," said Harry, "Because it kind of captures what racing seems to be all about. Except when it's not."

At that, Jack lifted his head up in kind of a jerk, almost as if to say *WHAAAATTT*??!!?

"Jack, have you also ever heard the phrase 'it's not if you win or lose, but how you play the game'?"

Jack again nodded his head yes.

"Tell me what that means to you Jack."

Jack answered "It means to play and race fairly, not cheat, follow the rules, not try to hurt someone, and to always do your very best."

"It's how I race every time, how I have always raced, but people still don't like me."

"And I guess the reason they do not like me is because they are jealous of me."

At this, Harry now nodded his head.

"Jack, these two sayings are the key to all you have been going through."

"And if we can get through them, that's where we will find the answers I think you are looking for."

Harry went on, and what he said next gave Jack lots to think about.

"It's not if you win or lose, but how you play the game. It's a phrase that became really popular, and for some very good reasons."

"But along the way, as time has gone on, like most everything else, people have lost its true meaning."

"Sure, everyone knows they should follow the rules, not cheat, not try to hurt anyone, always listen to their coaches."

"Everyone knows all of this but some still find ways to not do them."

"But that is not where everyone has lost what that phrase truly means."

"And that everyone includes you Jack."

Now this was something Jack was not expecting to hear, and something that really made him mad.

How dare he, thought Jack, *who does he think he is to tell me I don't race fairly!*

But before Jack could speak, Harry continued.

"Jack, I know this to be true because I did it too."

"And unfortunately for me, no one stopped to help me see where I was going wrong."

"But remember I told you there were going to be some things you did not want to hear, but could help you?"

"This is definitely one of those things, and something I wish someone had said to me, so may I please continue?"

And Jack, still upset, but also wanting to see and hear where Harry was going, nodded yes, but in an almost angry way.

"Okay, good," said Harry, "Let's get into what I discovered, and what I believe will help."

"Like I said before, how you play the game is a real accurate phrase."

"Except we all fall sadly short of all the phrase truly means."

"Getting past the rules and stuff, let's actually see how we can use this phrase that brings it to life, and makes everyone a better competitor, regardless of ability or speed."

"What how you play the game truly means is not about winning or losing, but how you do it."

"And by how I do it, you need to start looking at things from another perspective, by which I mean your fellow competitors' viewpoint."

"Jack, everyone knows you are the best and fastest. Everyone knows that you are most likely going to win, although you also need to know that eventually that will stop, as I discovered."

"But that really doesn't matter in the end. Because in the end, if you don't start making a change, the lack of friends you have now will be replaced with the ones I talked about earlier, who are only there when you win, and as I discovered, leave very quickly when you don't."

"So Jack, getting past all of the greatness you have inside of you, let me ask you a question."

"And it's going to be a question that may seem a little odd, but I want you to take some time and think about it before you answer."

"Can you do that Jack?"

And Jack again nodded his head yes.

"Okay, here we go."

"Jack, how do you do in school? What are your grades like?"

Jack answered a little slowly "I do okay."

"There are some classes I like, and some I don't, but I think I do okay."

"So Jack," said Harry, "Are there any others in your classes, both the ones you do like and the ones you don't, that do better than you?"

Jack answered even more slowly. "Yes, there are some kids that are real smart."

"It seems like school is super-easy for them, and they don't have to try very hard at school to get great grades...it actually seems unfair, because I try real hard at school but they just seem to be smarter than me, even in the classes I really like."

And again, this was Harry's turn to nod yes.

Harry said, "Yeah, I remember that too. There was always that one kid who everything in school came so easily to. It did seem unfair."

At that, they both sat still for a few seconds, thinking about school and how they worked hard, and how it seemed like there was always a kid that was just super-smart.

And then Harry again broke the silence, and what he said made Jack sit up straight.

"Jack, let's talk about those kids that are really smart."

"Do they talk about how they are going to ace every test?"

"Do they talk about how they don't have to study at night?"

"When they get their tests back, or when grades get posted, do they do back-flips, beat their chest, yell and point at themselves?"

"Of course not," said Jack "That would be weird, and it would make everyone else feel so bad..."

And as Jack trailed off, he realized the point Harry was making.

"Yes, that's right Jack. Go on," said Harry.

"But," said Jack, "That's different."

"I mean, it's school, and that's not the right place to do that."

"And it's completely different because that's only about how smart you are, not how hard you work."

As Jack finished, he looked at Harry uncertainly.

"Jack, do you really believe that?" spoke Harry.

"Do you really believe it's all so different?"

"Because what it really comes down too is something very simple."

"Each of us is uniquely gifted."

"Some of us are super-smart."

"Some of us are super fast."

"Some of us are great mechanics, and so on."

"But the important thing here is we are all gifted differently."

"That doesn't mean that you can't do well in school."

"Just like it doesn't mean that others should not race you."

"What it does mean is it's how we play the game, whatever that game is, how we do that will truly decide if we are winners."

"So when you are out racing, it may be true that you are going to dominate."

"Which is awesome, and something you should be proud of."

"But understand there is a big difference between being proud and prideful."

"And when you beat your chest and point fingers at yourself, and tell everyone how amazing you are, and how they are not, that's being prideful, and that is how you DON'T play the game."

And before Jack could say anything, Harry continued.

"I used the example of school to make a point Jack."

"And while it may seem silly to think about someone doing all of those things when school comes easy to them, I'll bet you have heard people brag about it."

"And I'll bet that didn't make you feel very good about yourself, or about them."

And Jack, remembering times when he had studied and tried his best on a test, only to not get a good grade, while others seemed to breeze through the class and made jokes about people that struggled in the class, nodded.

"Jack, you have to start seeing yourself as others see you in races."

"Everyone knows you are fast. And that you will most likely win."

"And while no one wants to lose, absolutely no one wants to be made to feel bad or like they don't matter."

"And this is the reason why no one wants to celebrate with you, or high five you, Jack."

"Because for a very long time now you have been making every-one feel like they are worthless,,,in fact, I believe you said they were wasting your time?"

As Harry said this Jack realized how ugly it sounded, and how ugly it must have looked, but even more than that, how ugly he must have started to appear to everyone.

"Jack, this is that point I talked about earlier. The thing you prob-ably did not want to hear, but needed to."

"And this is the one thing that you will need to change, so that true change can begin to happen slowly."

"How you play the game has to change now, Jack, or in the end you will wind up like me."

"Alone, lonely and forgotten, with nothing but empty trophies, ribbons and faded press clippings."

And as Jack listened to Harry speak, he knew he had a lot to think about.

Jack knew that change had to happen, because he really did miss all of his friends, and wanted more than ever to have that time back with them again.

But he did have a question for Harry.

"Harry," he asked, "Should I let someone else win?"

"Let someone else experience the joy I used to feel with winning."

And Harry replied "Jack, I get why you are asking that."

"It seems like the best thing to do."

"After all, it would be giving someone the gift that you have, to have them feel what you feel."

"But that is almost the worst thing you can do here, Jack."

"People are very smart, and they can tell when you are not trying your hardest."

"And as things are now, they will think you think they are not good enough, that you have to give them a win instead of them earning it, and that will just make them madder."

"Remember that it's how you play the game. And how you play the game means doing your absolute best in that moment, always honoring the gift you have been given."

And," Harry chuckled, "If you keep working hard to win, even though it seems easy, you will inspire others to work as hard, and then you really will have a race on your hands!"

And as Jack listened, he knew what Harry was saying was true. And he was grateful for the time Harry had spent with him, but he also felt sad at how lonely Harry seemed.

"Harry, thank you so much."

"What you said is so hard to hear, and it makes me sad that you went through all of this alone."

"I wish there was something I could do to make things better for you."

"Jack," Harry said, "I appreciate that."

"But what I want most from you now is for you to go out and make these changes."

"I will always be around, watching as a race fan."

"And if you ever need someone to talk with, I would be honored to be that person."

"The next steps are all up to you Jack."

"You decide, and keep deciding, how you want to play the game."

"It won't be easy, and people will not believe you right away, but if you stick with it, if you honestly congratulate others and run your races humbly, your true friends will eventually make their way back to you."

"But," warned Harry, "If you don't make these changes then you will end up like me."

"Remember the phrase "winning isn't everything, it's the only thing?"

"I learned the hard way how true that statement can be."

"When nothing else matters, winning does become the only thing."

"And that is a life as empty as the trophy cups you will win."

With that, Jack and Harry looked at each other for a long time, each with an expression of hope on their faces.

And soon, Jack began to ask Harry about his past, and about all his races, and the experiences Harry had around the world as a racer.

Which is where this story ends, so Jack and Harry can write another one.

As we leave Jack and Harry sitting under the moonlight talking, remember this.

In all things you do, whether sports or school or games or work or whatever, while doing your absolute best is always important, it's how you do your best and how you play the game you are in that truly matters.

As Jack learned, being a champion means far more than first place.

Live a champion life, and you will lead others to championships of their own.

And that is the Art of Winning.

ABOUT THE AUTHOR

D o you remember when you were young, and you were filled with dreams, hopes and aspirations?

Every kid had a dream about what they wanted to be when they grew up. Some wanted to be astronauts, some firemen or policemen, others wanted to be professional athletes, and the list goes on from there.

At some point though, the "growing up" occurs, and we start down paths we never knew existed when we were busy being kids.

Scott, like so many of us, has had an interesting path through life, but one thing has always remained the same since he was young: his love of books and reading.

Throughout his life, he has been able to see, experience and influence the direction and lives of many people, along with receiving equal amounts of guidance, mentorship and leadership. Along the way, his affinity for the water led him to compete as a college swimmer(5 years) and a college swim coach (20 years), while also serving and competing as a seasonal beach lifeguard (15 years).

Out of the water, Scott attended UC Irvine, graduating with a degree in Social Ecology with a minor in English. After graduation, since he did not know what he wanted to do, he went to Law School, attending the University of Utah College of Law (now S.J. Quinney

College of Law); yes, you can call him esquire, and no, he thankfully did not pass the bar. After graduating, he immediately made the best decision of his life, marrying Kristi, whom he met in his last year of college.

In 2011, after building a successful business with Kristi, Scott was able to retire from coaching to help grow not only their business, but also their marriage and pour into their two sons. They have both taken the opportunity to be active in their church and their sons' school, where among many things Kristi is the head track coach and Scott announces sports throughout the year.

Through all these life experiences, Scott has both knowingly and unknowingly been benefitting from the wisdom and advice of others, while also observing who people are and how they think and act. All of this time has led him back to what he dreamed of (and forgot) over 40 years ago in 1978 as a 5th grader;

I think someday I might want to be a writer.

After all this time, Scott has found his way back to what he dreamed of before he "grew up", and maybe you can too.

Coming Spring 2020
Volume 2
Bedtime Stories for a Lifetime of Leadership

CONNECT & FOLLOW

Facebook	@ScottMcGihonAuthor
Twitter	@scottmcgihonauthor
Instagram	@scottmcgihonauthor
email	scottmcgihonauthor@gmail.com